DISCOVER THE CELTS
AND THE IRON AGE

Warriors & Weapons

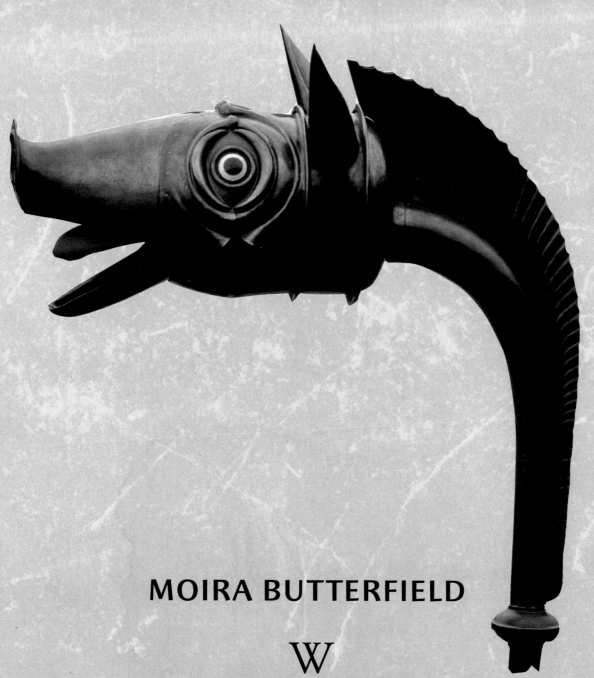

MOIRA BUTTERFIELD

W
FRANKLIN WATTS
LONDON·SYDNEY

Franklin Watts
First published in Great Britain in 2016 by The Watts Publishing Group

Credits
Series Editor: John C. Miles
Series Designer: Jane Hawkins
Picture researcher: Kathy Lockley

Picture credits: Alamy/C.M.Dixon/Heritage Image Partnership: 13 eye35 stock: 15
Werner Forman Archive/Heritage Image Partnership: COVER (Main), 6, 16
imageBROKER: 18 Alan King: 29 Lanmas: 24 David Lyons: Titlepage, 17
© The Trustees of the British Museum: 7
Chez Casver (Xuan Che)/ http://www.flickr.com/photos/rosemania/4121248502: 20
CORBIS/Jason Hawkes: 14 Getty Images/C.M. Dixon/Print Collector: 21B
Werner Forman Archive/Heritage Images: 11 Werner Forman/Universal Images: 8
Markus Matzel/Ullstein bild via Getty: 10 Patrick PIEL/Gamma-Rapho via Getty: 22B
National Museums of Scotland: 5 REX/Shutterstock/TONY BARTHOLOMEW: 23T
Shutterstock.com art_of_sun: Cover donatas1205: Cover meunierd: 26 Adrian Reynolds: 19
Topfoto.co.uk/ C.M. Dixon/HIP: 25, 27 Wikipedia/ Ealdgyth: 9 www.numismantica.com: 4

Every attempt has been made to clear copyright. Should there be any inadvertent omission please
apply to the publisher for rectification.

ISBN 978 1 4451 4816 8

Printed in China

Franklin Watts
An imprint of
Hachette Children's Group
Part of The Watts Publishing Group
Carmelite House
50 Victoria Embankment
London EC4Y 0DZ

An Hachette UK Company
www.hachette.co.uk

www.franklinwatts.co.uk

CONTENTS

MEET THE IRON AGE CELTS

Between 3,000 and 2,000 years ago northern Europe was a dangerous place. We call this warlike period the Iron Age and we call the people who lived across northern Europe at this time the Celts. The end of the Iron Age in Britain came when the ancient Romans took control. They defeated Celtic tribes in battle and the way that people lived then began to change.

BETTER METAL

The Iron Age gets its name because it was a time when people began to use iron tools and weapons instead of bronze ones. Around 800 BCE the secret of making iron came to Britain from Europe, marking the beginning of the British Iron Age. Iron was cheaper and easier to make than bronze and it was more hard-wearing. It made much better weapons and farming equipment.

MEET THE PEOPLE

Iron Age Celts did not write anything down themselves but ancient Greek and Roman writers described them. We know that they lived in tribes led by chieftains and warriors. They

WAS THERE A KING OF BRITAIN IN IRON AGE TIMES?

No. There were many local chieftains. Nobody would have understood the idea of one country called Britain, led by one person.

were fierce fighters who rode to war in horse-drawn chariots. The Celtic tribes fought between themselves for land and cattle, and when the Romans came some of them fought the new invaders rather than give in and let them rule.

FINDING THE WEAPONS

We know about some of the weapons that Iron Age fighters used because a few of them have turned up in graves. Iron Age chieftains and warriors were sometimes buried along with their fighting equipment, perhaps to use in an afterlife.

War weapons, such as swords and shields, have also been discovered in rivers and lakes. The Celts probably threw them in as offerings to their gods and goddesses.

FROM THE IRON AGE

This Iron Age cap was made for a pony, perhaps to wear into battle. The pony would have looked impressive with its iron horns. The owner threw it into a Scottish peat bog, possibly as an offering to the gods.

◀ The pony cap is in the National Museum of Scotland in Edinburgh.

TOP IN THE TRIBE

During the Iron Age different tribes ruled different areas around Britain, led by their warrior chieftains. Each tribe controlled their own territory and fought other tribes for land and wealth.

TRIBAL CHIEFS

A tribe was a clan linked together by family connections. Each tribe was led by a chief backed up by bands of warriors. Everyone had to obey the chiefs, who could be women as well as men.

▲ This decorated Iron Age cauldron shows a band of Celtic fighters.

We know from Roman writing that there were over thirty tribes living in Britain at the end of the Iron Age.

LEADERS AND FOLLOWERS

Ordinary Iron Age Britons spent their days farming - growing crops and looking after animals to feed their families. They owned very little, and when they died they were not buried with treasures. Their tribal chief and his best warriors would have owned more than them. Chiefs rewarded their faithful warriors with horses and weapons, and later on in the Iron Age they began paying them with gold coins.

DIRECTED BY DRUIDS

The tribal chiefs listened to the advice of priests called Druids. They told the chiefs when to fight and thought they could predict the future using magical rituals. The Celts believed in many gods and goddesses, some of them gods of war. Before a battle the Druids may have led ceremonies to get the gods on their side, sacrificing animals and sometimes even people to please them.

WHO WERE THE CHIEFS?

We know the names of some chiefs the Romans met when they arrived to conquer Britain. Two of them were women – Boudicca (Queen of the Iceni in eastern England) and Cartimandua (Queen of the Brigantes in northern England).

FROM THE IRON AGE

This skull of a man comes from an Iron Age grave in Deal, Kent. He was buried with a bronze crown, a sword and shield. He may have been a chief or an important Druid.

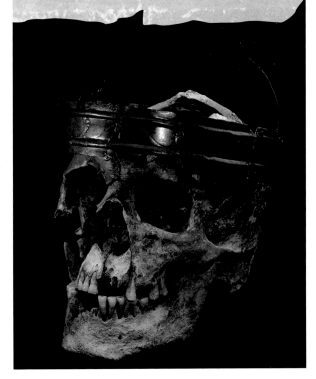

WARRIORS' WEAPONS

Iron Age warriors fought on foot or in chariots (see p18). They carried spears and shields, and some fought with slingshots. Swords were very highly prized. They belonged to the wealthiest, most important warriors.

LEADER'S SWORD

Celtic swords were around 70-90 cm long. They were designed for slashing at the enemy. One of the finest Iron Age swords found so far came from a grave in Kirkburn, Yorkshire. We don't know who owned it, but it was made with great skill from seventy different parts. The owner had it repaired at some point. Perhaps it was damaged in battle but was too precious to throw away. It was kept in a decorated metal scabbard, which would have impressed everyone who saw it.

SPEARS AND SLINGSHOTS

Most warriors used spears, which they threw like javelins. They must have spent time practising their spear-throwing to make

FROM THE IRON AGE

The Kirkburn sword was buried with an important man, perhaps a chieftain. It's possible that the decorations on the sword were magical charms meant to protect the swordsman.

◄ This Celtic bronze sword hilt (handle) is made in the shape of a human figure. It dates from the 1st century BCE.

themselves expert. We know they also fired stones from a slingshot - a leather pouch with straps. The stone was put in the slingshot pouch, whirled around and launched. It could fly fast and hit hard, but the slingshot user would need lots of skill to aim it. Piles of slingshot stones have been found in Iron Age hill forts, ready to use in war and perhaps for hunting animals, too.

SHIELDS AND HELMETS

Most shields were made of wood or leather and they have rotted away, leaving only the metal centre behind, called the boss. A few decorated shields have turned up, but they were probably made for show - to use in ceremonies, not battles. Helmets are incredibly rare to find, and we know very little about them, but one very unusual one was dredged up from under Waterloo Bridge in London, in 1868. It had metal horns! It might have been made for a ceremony, too, but we don't know for sure.

An Iron Age horned helmet found in the River Thames, under Waterloo Bridge in London. ▶

WHAT DID WARRIORS LOOK LIKE?

Celtic warriors were known for being incredibly brave but also very proud of their appearance. They went into battle looking as fearsome and as impressive as they could.

SAVED BY A SHIELD

Some Celtic warriors wore helmets and an early type of chainmail, but most just wore breeches and tunics. According to their Roman enemies some even went into battle wearing nothing at all - only their weapon belt and a gleaming neck ring called a torc. Having little or no armour meant the Celts had to rely heavily on their rectangular-shaped shields. If they lost their shield they would be in great danger on a battlefield.

BLUE BRAVERY

Before a battle the Celtic warriors apparently painted themselves blue. They probably used blue colour extracted from a plant called woad. Not only did it make them look scary to their enemies, it was antiseptic and helped to heal skin wounds. It's possible they painted

WHAT DID CHIEFS WEAR?

We don't know for sure. This German statue of a Celtic leader is a very rare example. It dates to 500 BCE. It has a shield, a torc and a strange-looking headdress.

magical protective symbols on themselves, too - body art especially for battle.

LOOKING GOOD

The Roman writer Strabo tells us that the Celts were very proud of their physique. He said they tried hard not to get pot-bellied, and if a young man was judged to be getting too fat he was punished, though it's not clear how. They wore their hair long and they had long moustaches, too. Sometimes they plaited their hair or even plastered it with lime-wash or clay to make it stick out like a flying mane.

FROM THE IRON AGE

This head is from a famous Roman statue called 'Dying Gaul'. The Gauls were Celtic tribes who lived in France. The fighter is wearing a neck torc, which would have been made from gold, silver and bronze.

This Roman statue of a Celt is shown with spiky hair. Celts rubbed their hair with clay or lime-wash. ▼

WHO FOUGHT WHO?

Celtic tribes often fought each other for power and wealth. Farmland, farm animals and horses would have been the prizes of victory, along with the wives and children of defeated warriors.

NEVER UNITED

Celtic tribes were always arguing amongst themselves. They sometimes had alliances, but they couldn't be relied on and they often changed sides. There was treachery, murder and ancient feuds between families. Some tribes were sworn enemies. For instance, the Trinovantes, based in the Suffolk and Essex area, always hated their neighbours to the west, the Catuvellauni. When the Romans arrived to take over Britain in CE 43 the two tribes could not bring themselves to fight together against the invader.

DYKE DEFENCES

Some tribes dug big ditches and banks we call dykes to keep out neighbouring enemies from their territory. The Celtic settlement of Camulodunum - now Colchester - had dykes 24 km long and up to 7.6 m deep, probably created by the Trinovantes to stop the chariots of the hated Catuvellauni. They don't seem to have worked around 55 BCE, when the Catuvellauni attacked and killed the King of the Trinovantes.

DEATH AND SLAVERY

Losing to another tribe meant death for warriors. The families of the defeated might be taken as slaves and faced a tough future of being owned by someone. Later in the Iron Age slaves were sold abroad, so defeat in battle could mean leaving Britain for good.

BLOODTHIRSTY VICTORS

The Celts liked to cut off the heads of their defeated enemies and display them, dangling them from their horses as they rode home after a victory.

FROM THE IRON AGE

Heads were religious objects for Celts, so they took those of their enemies. These eerie-looking pillars, decorated with skulls, come from the entrance to a Celtic religious shrine in Roquepertuse, near modern-day Marseille in France.

Perhaps the skulls at the shrine belonged to defeated enemies. ▼

HIDING IN A HILL FORT

Some tribes hid inside hill forts - settlements high up on hilltops surrounded by high banks and deep ditches to keep enemies out.

FROM THE IRON AGE

Danebury hill fort in Hampshire was home to Iron Age people for 500 years. Archaeologists have found human remains there that show battle injuries from swords and spears.

People living high on Danebury could see their enemies coming. ▼

STRONGHOLDS UP HIGH

There were hundreds of hill forts around Britain. Tribal leaders used them as strongholds, living in them with their warriors and families. Some hill forts were large enough for hundreds of people, with lots of huts, pits for storing grain, animal pens and religious shrines hidden inside the defensive walls.

ATTACK!

It would be easy to see an enemy coming from high up in a hill fort. Once the alarm was raised everybody would rush inside and the gate would be shut. Defenders would then hurl down stones and spears on attackers as they tried to breach the gate. Archaeologists have found that the hill fort at Danebury in Hampshire once had its gates burnt down, perhaps during an attack.

WHEN HILL FORTS FELL

Grisly finds at Fin Cop hill fort in Derbyshire give us some idea of what might have happened if a hill fort was conquered. Sadly for the people of Fin Cop, disaster struck around 390 BCE.

HOW MANY PEOPLE COULD HIDE IN A HILL FORT?

A big hill fort, such as Danebury, had room for 300–400 people.

▲ Banks and ditches of Fin Cop hill fort, where a massacre took place.

They hurriedly tried to build a hill fort but it seems they hadn't finished it when an attack came. They were defeated, massacred and thrown into a ditch, where archaeologists found their skeletons, including women and young children.

NOISY FIGHTERS

Celtic warriors were very brave, and very noisy when they went into battle. They deliberately made lots of noise to scare their enemies.

DEATH OR GLORY

Roman writers said that the Celts loved war and were quick to fight. The Celts saw death in battle as a glorious thing, and they were very brave. But though courageous, they were easily outwitted by wily Roman battle-tactics (according to the boastful Romans). Young Celtic warriors trained from an early age with their friends and fought together for death or glory.

CHARGE!

Most warriors fought on foot. At the beginning of a battle they waved their swords, banged their shields, sang war songs and blew war horns. They wanted to frighten their enemy with noise and a show of strength, like a rugby team doing a haka war dance. Then everyone rushed forwards, screaming and throwing spears. They crashed into the enemy, slashing with their swords.

FROM THE IRON AGE

This coin, made for a chief of the Catuvellauni tribe, shows a horseman carrying a carnyx. You can also see three more on page 6.

REGROUPING

If the first charge failed they would regroup and charge again and again, but if they had to retreat they tended to be disorganised. That's when they were most vulnerable to being wiped out.

HORRIBLE HORNS

A Celtic war horn, called a carnyx, was a 1-2-m long tube of beaten bronze with an animal head on the end. Different tribes may have had different animal heads, such as a wolf, horse or snake. The horns made a terrifying loud noise, especially when lots of them were played together at the beginning of a battle. It's possible the Celts thought the noise could call up their gods to help them. Horn sounds were used to give commands on the battlefield, too.

▲ A carnynx boar's head

WHAT DID WAR HORNS LOOK LIKE?

This reconstruction is based on a carnyx boar's head found on the shores of a Scottish Loch. It's called the Deskford Carnyx, and it was probably thrown in the water as an offering to the gods. It had a wooden tongue that moved when it was blown.

TO WAR IN CHARIOTS

When not fighting on foot, Celtic warriors fought in chariots or on horseback. Chariots were popular in late Iron Age times. As well as battles they were used for everyday transport and probably for racing, too.

▲ A reconstruction of a Celtic war chariot in an Austrian museum.

EXPERT TEAM

Onboard a chariot there would be one driver and one warrior ready to throw spears or to jump down and fight. Celtic warriors must have been good horsemen because they didn't have stirrups

HOW FAST DID IRON AGE CHARIOTS GO?

They probably had a top speed of around 32 kph (20 mph).

to help keep them in the saddle when riding. Stirrups hadn't been invented yet! The chariot drivers had to be skilled, too. They had to control their chariot at full gallop and turn quickly on the battlefield.

The chariot pole was a long piece of wood to which the horses were harnessed. Apparently warriors sometimes stood on the chariot pole and ran down to the horses and back, to show off their bravery at the beginning of a battle.

TWO-WHEELED TRANSPORT

Iron Age chariots had two wheels and two horses, and the Celts liked them to look good, with brightly decorated bronze horse equipment. Small metal chariot parts have been found scattered all over Britain, including over 100 wheel linchpins. Accidents must sometimes have happened, because if a linchpin fell out a wheel would fall off!

FOR THE GODS

It seems that the Celts valued their chariots so much they sometimes gave them to the gods. Archaeologists exploring an ancient Celtic village near Melton Mowbray in Leicestershire found a set of chariot parts that had been carefully put in a box, then ceremonially burnt in a pit. When the owners burnt it they had a feast and threw food bones and other precious possessions into the pit, too. They may have wanted to please the gods by giving them fine things.

FROM THE IRON AGE

This Victorian statue in London shows Queen Boudicca of the Iceni tribe in a war chariot. It shows blades sticking out of the wheels, but nobody knows if Celtic war chariots had these for sure.

A VICTORY FEAST

When Iron Age Celts returned from a victory they celebrated with a big feast thrown by the leaders for their warriors.

WINNER'S DINNER

The man judged to be the bravest fighter was given the best roasted joint of pork as a mark of his success. The meat was roasted on a spit over a fire, with spectacular-looking poles at either end called fire dogs, decorated with magical-looking creatures. They were a sign that the feast was an important event. The very best meat and drink was probably served as a reward for winning.

CHAMPION DRINKERS

A singing poet called a bard would sing and tell tales of daring deeds as the warriors feasted and drank wine and mead (an alcoholic drink made from honey). The Romans said that the Celts were big drinkers! During a feast they would fill ceremonial buckets and cauldrons with alcohol and drink it from the horns of aurochs, wild cattle much bigger than the cattle we have today.

▶ This huge drinking horn comes from the grave of an Iron Age chieftain who lived in Germany. He was buried with nine drinking horns and a cauldron full of alcohol. This horn holds 5.5 litres (10 pints) of liquid.

PILE FOR THE GODS

The victors would bring home war booty - valuable goods and prisoners-of-war. Some tribes gave booty to their gods, piling it up near religious shrines set up in sacred outdoor groves of trees. The mounds lay untouched for generations, and if anyone was discovered stealing from the pile of the gods they were punished with death. It's possible that animals and even human captives were sacrificed to the gods as a 'thank you' for victory.

DID THE IRON AGE CELTS REALLY SACRIFICE PRISONERS-OF-WAR TO THEIR GODS?

We don't know. The Romans said they did, but the Romans were their enemies. We can't be sure they were telling the whole truth.

FROM THE IRON AGE

This fire dog is from Wales. Do you think the magical-looking animal is a horse, a bull or perhaps a mythical beast?

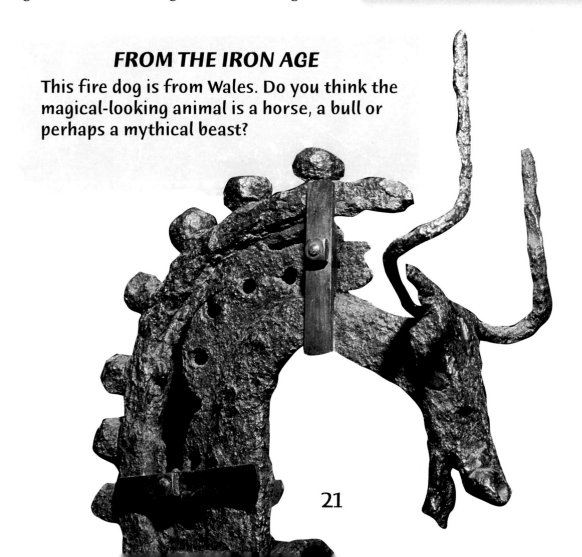

21

GRAVES OF POWER

Iron Age warrior graves are rare to find. Only the most important warriors got a burial, it seems. The warriors were buried with their weapons and sometimes their chariots, too.

WHY BREAK A SWORD?

Around 74-25 BCE, just over 2,000 years ago, a Late Iron Age warrior was buried overlooking a village at Kelvedon in Essex. The warrior's body has not survived - but we know he was a fighter because he had a sword, scabbard, dagger, spear and shield. His sword and spear were deliberately bent before they were buried with him. Deliberately broken weapons have been found in other parts of the Celtic world, too. Nobody knows why, but there are two theories. What do you think?

- The weapons were ritually 'killed' to send them into the afterlife with their owner.

- The weapons were bent to stop the owner coming back as an angry spirit.

FROM THE IRON AGE

Some warrior graves are a little different. This dagger and sheath was found in the grave of a German chieftain. Before it was buried it was improved, not bent. It was coated with gold leaf (reconstructed here) for a really showy effect.

RIDING ON

It seems that Celtic chieftains and warriors were expected to rule in the afterlife, too. They were buried with the things they needed to impress and stay in power. In some cases they were even buried with chariots. One chariot burial in Wetwang, Yorkshire, turned out to be the grave of a woman, perhaps an important tribal ruler similar to Boudicca.

PIGS GO TOO

When important Iron Age people such as warriors were buried, they were often given a roasted joint of pig meat to take with them to the other world. The gods were said to enjoy roast pig. In an ancient Irish Celtic story, the gods

▲ A chariot burial being studied by archaeologists in Yorkshire.

of the afterworld threw feasts, and all the pigs that were killed and eaten were magically reborn to be eaten over and over again!

ARE ALL IRON AGE WEAPONS THE SAME?

Definitely not! Over time and in different places there were fashions for different shaped swords and shields. Some of them look so fancy they were probably used in ceremonies, not for fighting at all.

23

ROMANS V. CELTS

In 55 BCE the first Roman ships appeared on the coast of Britain. Brilliant Roman General Julius Caesar had conquered the Celtic Gauls in France and was now taking a look at the strange foggy island to the north!

THE FIRST LANDING

The Romans had executed many Celtic leaders in Gaul but some of them escaped and fled to Britain, so the Britons would have heard about the formidable Roman army. When Caesar's fleet arrived near Dover the southern English tribes joined up to scare them off.

WHAT DID THE ROMANS THINK OF THE BRITONS?

Julius Caesar called the Britons barbarians. To the Romans, they were savages living on the fringes of the world.

24

Chariots raced along the shore, and churned up the water, while warriors screamed insults and threw their spears. At first the Roman soldiers were too cautious to come ashore, but they eventually landed and drove the Britons back.

FRIENDS AND ENEMIES

Some southern English tribes did deals with Caesar, promising to pay him tribute (taxes). Others tried to fight but were defeated and forced to agree peace. There was treachery between the tribes, most notably between those arch-enemies the Catuvellauni and the Trinovantes. The Trinovantes made a peace deal with Caesar while the Catuvellauni tried to fight them. Caesar and his army left Britain in 54 BCE knowing that the Romans had allies there.

THE ROMANS RETURN

In CE 43 the Roman army returned, this time sent by Emperor Claudius. Britain had valuable metals, such as silver and tin, plus lots of useful farmland. It also had rebellious tribes who were defying Rome, so Claudius decided it was time to take over for good. He sent

nearly 50,000 Roman troops, who drove Celtic forces back and took the tribal base of Camulodunum - now Colchester.

FROM THE IRON AGE

This gravestone from Camulodunum is the earliest Roman sculpture found in Britain. It comes from around the time of the CE 43 invasion. It shows Roman soldier Longinus riding over a defeated Briton.

FIGHTING BACK

Many English and Welsh tribes tried to stop the advance of the invading Romans, but although the warriors fought with great bravery they were no match for the well-drilled Roman army, who had better armour and equipment.

▲ Re-enactors show how the Roman soldiers used their shields to deflect Celtic spears.

WHY DID THE CELTIC WARRIORS LOSE TO THE ROMANS?

The Celtic warriors knew how to fight each other, but not the well-trained Roman army, who fought in a much more disciplined way. The Iron Age way of fighting was over.

DEFEATED IN THE HILL FORTS

Roman troops marched across England, demanding that the tribes agree to give Rome their loyalty. Some tribes refused and hid in their hill forts. The Romans used big bolt-firing and stone-firing catapults called ballista to drive the defending Celts off the fort walls. Meanwhile, holding their shields up to protect themselves from spears and stones, Roman troops were able to reach the walls and break through, burning down the wooden fort gates. Roman ballista bolts have been found at some hill forts, evidence of the violent battles that took place.

CARATACUS BETRAYED

The Celts had their best successes against the Romans when they ambushed a small number of Roman troops and then escaped quickly. But in big battles the Romans had the upper hand. The Celts' best war leader was the chief of the Catuvellauni, Caratacus. In CE 51 he lost a vital battle on a hillside overlooking the River Severn. He fled north but was betrayed and handed over to the Romans by Cartimandua, Queen of the Brigantes. He was taken off to Rome in chains.

TROUBLE AGAIN

Angered by Roman brutality and land-grabbing, the Iceni and the Trinovante tribes rebelled in CE 60, led by Queen Boudicca. They destroyed Roman Colchester, St. Alban's and London, but at the Battle of Watling Street thousands of Celtic warriors were killed and the rebellion was crushed. It's not clear how Boudicca died. Some said she poisoned herself. For years afterwards there were still attacks from the Celts in Wales, but finally the Romans gained control of southern Britain.

FROM THE IRON AGE

This pot of silver Iceni tribe coins comes from a hoard of 872 coins buried in Cambridgeshire at the time of Boudicca's revolt. Perhaps someone was hiding their treasure for safety. If so, they never returned to collect it.

NOT GONE, BUT DIFFERENT

Roman forces governed southern England and Wales for around 400 years. Life changed greatly for ordinary people, and warriors were no longer needed. Instead the Roman army kept the peace.

ALL CHANGE

Under the Romans people in England and Wales began to live differently. They worshipped different gods and ate different foods, for instance. Some of them would have learnt to speak and write Latin, the language of the Romans. We call these people the Romano-British, not the Celts. The British tribal leaders who were friendly to Rome helped to rule, and began living in Roman-style luxury. However, the Scottish and Irish Celtic tribes were never Romanized. They continued to live in clans, with their own warriors and chiefs.

WARRIORS GONE

There was no need for warriors in parts of Britain ruled by the Romans. Instead Romano-British men could join the Roman Army as auxiliaries - the name

IS THERE ANYTHING I CAN SEE FROM THE IRON AGE?

You could visit an Iron Age hill fort. There are lots all over Britain. Stand on the top of the hill and imagine the Romans coming!

for troops who were not born in Rome. They could be sent anywhere in the Roman Empire, and eventually they could become Roman citizens.

Things changed once again when the Roman Empire fell apart. The Roman army left Britain in CE 410 and new invaders began to arrive from across the North

Sea. The Romano-British found it hard to fight back and the Anglo-Saxons soon took over much of southern England.

MAGIC LEFT BEHIND

The Iron Age Celtic warriors are gone, but some of the stories from those times are remembered. In Ireland and Wales, especially, ancient myths of fighting heroes survive. One Welsh legend tells of the 13 treasures of Britain, including a magical sword that could burst into flame, a cauldron that only cooked for brave men, a drinking horn that could make any drink appear and a chariot that could go at magical speed. That sounds like perfect equipment for the Iron Age warrior chiefs of old!

FROM THE IRON AGE? NO!

This carved stone comes from Inverness in Scotland. It shows a Pictish warrior drinking from a horn, and dates to around CE 900, hundreds of years after the Celtic tribes had been crushed in England. In Scotland and Ireland Celtic tribal life survived for centuries.

29

GLOSSARY

Afterlife The belief that there is another life in a heavenly place after death.

Antiseptic A substance that helps prevent the spread of disease.

Aurochs A breed of wild cattle that lived in Iron Age times. Aurochs were much bigger than modern cattle.

Auxiliaries Roman army soldiers who were not Roman citizens.

Ballista Big wooden catapults used by the Roman army.

Bard A singing poet who entertained tribal chiefs.

Blacksmith Someone who makes objects from metal.

Boss A round metal circle in the middle of a shield.

Carnyx A long bronze war horn.

Celts The name we now give to people who lived in Britain and Northern Europe between 3,000 and 2,000 years ago.

Clan A group of people linked together by family loyalty.

Druids Priests who advised Celtic tribal leaders and believed they could predict the future.

Dyke A big V-shaped ditch with high banks, dug to keep out an enemy.

Fire dogs Decorated poles at either end of a spit for roasting meat on a fire.

Grove A row of trees.

Hill fort A stronghold high up on a hill top, surrounded by defences.

Mead An alcoholic drink made from honey.

Picts Celtic tribes who lived in Scotland.

Ritual A religious ceremony.

Romano-British Britons who lived under Ancient Roman rule.

Scabbard A covering for a sword.

Sheath A leather or metal pouch for a dagger.

Shrine A holy place, often marked by a building or other construction.

Slingshot A leather pouch with a strap, for firing a stone.

Territory Land controlled by one group of people.

Torc A metal neck ring.

Woad A plant used to make blue-coloured body paint.

SOME IRON AGE WEBSITES

Take a look at some fabulous Iron Age torcs discovered in Scotland. Then design your own version!
http://www.nms.ac.uk/explore/collections-stories/scottish-history-and-archaeology/iron-age-gold-torcs/

A list of Iron Age sites you can visit around Britain.
http://www.bbc.co.uk/history/ancient/british_prehistory/ironage_sites_01.shtml

A list of museums around Britain with Iron Age objects to see.
http://www.schoolsprehistory.co.uk/2015/04/29/museums-with-stone-age-to-iron-age-collections-on-display/

Play some Welsh warrior games.
http://www.bbc.co.uk/wales/celts/

See some of the Iron age weapons kept at the British Museum.
http://www.britishmuseum.org/explore/highlights/article_index/w/weapons_and_warriors_in_iron_a.aspx

Note to parents and teachers: Every effort has been made by the Publishers to ensure that the websites in this book are suitable for children, that they are of the highest educational value, and that they contain no inappropriate or offensive material. However, because of the nature of the Internet, it is impossible to guarantee that the contents of these sites will not be altered. We strongly advise that Internet access is supervised by a responsible adult.

TIMELINE

800 BCE Iron-making spread to Britain, and the period we call the Iron Age began (replacing the Bronze Age).

700 BCE The first hill forts were built.

500-100 BCE The biggest hill forts were built.

330 BCE Greek explorer Pytheas sailed round Britain. He was the first person in history to write about the country.

300 BCE Celtic craftsmen began to decorate objects with swirling patterns.

100 BCE Coins were used for the first time, but only in the southeast.

55 BCE Ancient Romans troops arrived in Britain for the first time, under Julius Caesar.

CE 43 The ancient Romans returned to conquer southern Britain and Wales (not Scotland or Ireland).

CE 60 Tribes rebelled in southern Britain, led by Boudicca.

INDEX